Isaac Asimov's 21st Century Library of the Universe

The Solar System

Neptune

BY ISAAC ASIMOV

WITH REVISIONS AND UPDATING BY RICHARD HANTULA

Gareth Stevens Publishing
A WORLD ALMANAC EDUCATION GROUP COMPANY

Please visit our web site at: www.garethstevens.com
For a free color catalog describing Gareth Stevens Publishing's list of high-quality
books and multimedia programs, call 1-800-542-2595 (USA) or 1-800-387-3178 (Canada).
Gareth Stevens Publishing's fax: (414) 332-3567.

Library of Congress Cataloging-in-Publication Data

Asimov, Isaac.
    Neptune / by Isaac Asimov; with revisions and updating by Richard Hantula.
        p. cm. − (Isaac Asimov's 21st century library of the universe. The solar system)
    Rev. ed. of: Distant giant: the planet Neptune. 1996.
    Summary: Introduces the fourth largest known planet in the solar system.
    Includes bibliographical references and index.
    ISBN 0-8368-3239-6 (lib. bdg.)
    1. Neptune (Planet)−Juvenile literature. [1. Neptune (Planet).] I. Hantula, Richard.
II. Asimov, Isaac. Distant giant: the planet Neptune. III. Title. IV. Isaac Asimov's 21st
century library of the universe. Solar system.
    QB691.A83 2002
    523.48'1−dc21   2002021684

This edition first published in 2002 by
Gareth Stevens Publishing
A World Almanac Education Group Company
330 West Olive Street, Suite 100
Milwaukee, WI 53212 USA

Series editor: Betsy Rasmussen
Cover design and layout adaptation: Melissa Valuch
Picture research: Matthew Groshek
Additional picture research: Diane Laska-Swanke
Production director: Susan Ashley

The editors at Gareth Stevens Publishing have selected science author Richard Hantula to bring
this classic series of young people's information books up to date. Richard Hantula has written
and edited books and articles on science and technology for more than two decades. He was the
senior U.S. editor for the *Macmillan Encyclopedia of Science*.

In addition to Hantula's contribution to this most recent edition, the editors would like to
acknowledge the participation of two noted science authors, Greg Walz-Chojnacki and
Francis Reddy, as contributors to earlier editions of this work.

Printed in the United States of America

1 2 3 4 5 6 7 8 9 06 05 04 03 02

Contents

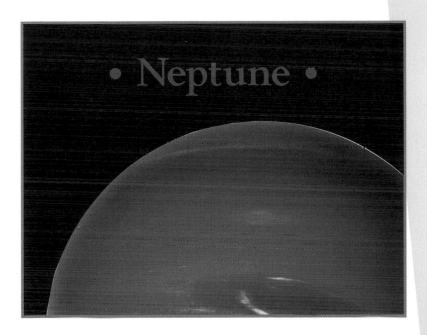

We live in an enormously large place − the Universe. It is only natural that we would want to understand this place, so scientists and engineers have developed instruments and spacecrafts that have told us far more about the Universe than we could possibly imagine.

We have seen planets up close, and spacecrafts have even landed on some. We have learned about quasars and pulsars, super-novas and colliding galaxies, and black holes and dark matter. We have gathered amazing data about how the Universe may have come into being and how it may end. Nothing could be more astonishing.

The giant blue world known as Neptune lacks a solid surface and is racked by powerful storms. It is the most distant planet in the Solar System that has been explored by a spacecraft. A probe called *Voyager 2* passed close to Neptune and its largest moon, Triton, in 1989 and sent back to Earth abundant data and pictures. Additional remarkable images have been produced by the Hubble Space Telescope and other instruments.

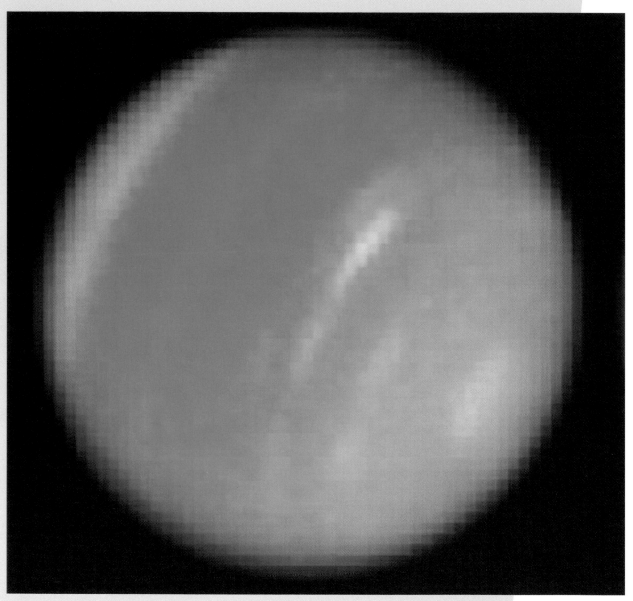

Above: An almost true-color image of Neptune taken by the Hubble Space Telescope.

Neptune's Discovery

By the 1840s, it was clear to scientists that the motion of Uranus (the most distant planet then known) was not what they considered normal.

Two researchers, John Couch Adams of England and Urbain Jean Joseph Leverrier of France, worked separately trying to explain this unusual motion. Each felt there must be a planet beyond Uranus that pulled at it and affected its motion. Each astronomer calculated where he thought this planet might be.

In 1846, two German astronomers, Johann Gottfried Galle and Heinrich Ludwig d'Arrest, observed the sky in the area where Leverrier predicted this planet would be — and they found it. The bluish planet was named Neptune after the Roman god of the sea. All four men — Galle, d'Arrest, Adams, and Leverrier — share credit in the discovery of Neptune.

Left: British astronomer John Couch Adams.

Right: French mathematician Urbain Jean Joseph Leverrier.

One of the Giants

There are four giant planets — Jupiter, Saturn, Uranus, and Neptune. Neptune is the most distant from Earth and the smallest of the four. It is still enormous, however, and measures about 30,760 miles (49,500 kilometers) across — four times wider than Earth. Its orbit lies, on average, about 2.8 billion miles (4.5 billion km) from the Sun — 30 times farther from the Sun than Earth is.

From Neptune, the Sun looks like a very bright star. Neptune gets only $1/900$ of the light and warmth from the Sun that Earth receives. Even so, sunshine on Neptune is 450 times brighter than light reflected to Earth from a full Moon.

Neptune orbits the Sun about once every 165 Earth years. A day on Neptune is a little over 16 hours long.

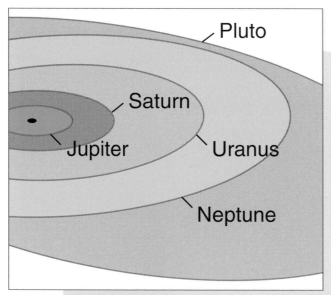

Left: The orbits of the five outer-most planets of our Solar System. Within Jupiter's orbit are the orbits of Mars, Earth, Venus, and Mercury. A small part of Pluto's orbit (not shown here) lies within Neptune's.

Which planet is the fastest of them all?

Earth travels around the Sun at 18.6 miles (29.9 km) per second. That is much faster than even our fastest rockets travel. The farther a planet is from the Sun, the weaker the Sun's gravitational pull on it and the slower the planet moves. Neptune is so distant from the Sun that it moves along its orbit at a speed of only 3.3 miles (5.3 km) per second. Mercury, the planet nearest the Sun, speeds along at an average rate of nearly 30 miles (48 km) per second.

Unlike Earth *(inset)*, which is one of the Solar System's "rocky" planets, Neptune is mostly gas and liquid and has no solid surface.

A false-color picture of Neptune based on *Voyager 2* data. Different colors represent different heights in Neptune's atmosphere. Lower clouds are shown darker in color and higher clouds lighter.

Triton and Nereid

Soon after Neptune was discovered, astronomers found a moon circling it. This moon, or satellite, was named Triton, after the son of Poseidon, the sea god of ancient Greek myths.

Triton is large with a diameter of 1,680 miles (2,700 km), which is about 78 percent the diameter of Earth's Moon. Triton is about the same distance from Neptune as Earth's Moon is from Earth. Triton circles Neptune in just under six days. Earth's Moon circles Earth in just over 27 1/3 days. Triton takes less time to complete one orbit, because Neptune is larger than Earth and has a stronger gravitational pull.

In 1949, a second moon, Nereid, was discovered. It is about 210 miles (340 km) across and is much farther from Neptune than Triton – over 15 times as far, on average. It takes Nereid 360 days to orbit Neptune. This is almost as long as it takes Earth to orbit the Sun.

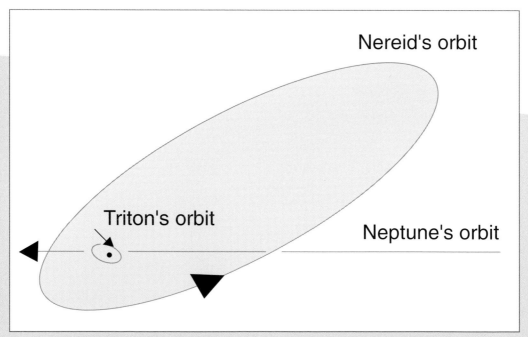

Above: Nereid has an extremely oval orbit. Unlike most of the Solar System's moons, Triton orbits Neptune in the opposite direction of Neptune's rotation. The orbits of both Triton and Nereid are tilted at an angle to Neptune's equator. The straight line shows the direction of Neptune's path around the Sun.

Above: This photograph of Triton's speckled surface was taken by *Voyager 2.*

Inset: Triton *(top arrow)* and Nereid *(bottom arrow)* are moons in orbit around Neptune.

9

Neptune's second-largest known satellite, Proteus, is a gray cratered ball. Before *Voyager 2* detected Proteus, Nereid was thought to be Neptune's second-largest moon.

Inset: *Voyager 2* has provided the only detailed glimpse of Proteus. Scientists can use these pictures to make maps. In this map, Proteus is split in two – the half that leads the way in the moon's orbit around Neptune and the half that follows.

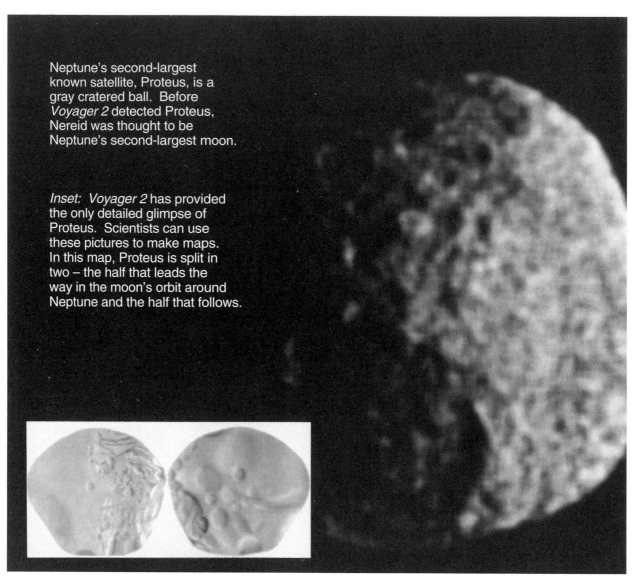

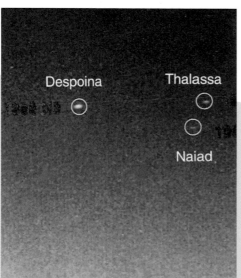

Left: Three of Neptune's six "new" moons from a *Voyager 2* image.

Despoina

Thalassa

Naiad

New Moons

When *Voyager 2* flew near Neptune in 1989, it spotted six more satellites orbiting the planet. These moons are all quite close to Neptune. Their widths, or diameters, are estimated to range from 30 to 260 miles (50 to 420 km). They reflect only small amounts of light. Their darkness, small size, and great distance from Earth makes them difficult to observe from Earth.

Like all the other known small satellites in the Solar System, Neptune's newly discovered moons are lumpy and irregular. Only large celestial bodies have enough gravitational force to form a round shape.

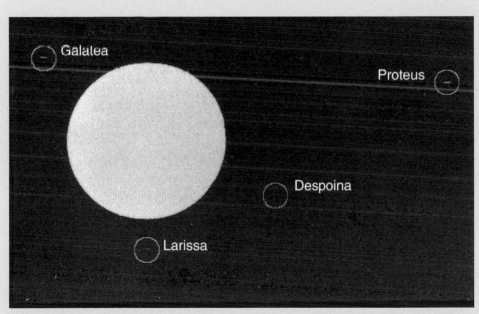

Above: Four of Neptune's six "new" moons from a *Voyager 2* image. Despoina is shown in this image and the image on the opposite page.

Neptune Has Rings

From their viewpoint on Earth, astronomers observed that when Neptune moved toward a star, the star's light dimmed a little just before Neptune covered it. This was a clue to scientists that there might be rings around Neptune. The rings did not seem to be complete, however. They appeared to be more like arcs, or pieces of rings.

As *Voyager 2* passed Neptune, it revealed that there are four complete rings around the planet. They are thin, without much material in them, and clumpy. The clumps hide the stars more than other parts of the rings do. That is why the rings looked like arcs, rather than full rings, from Earth.

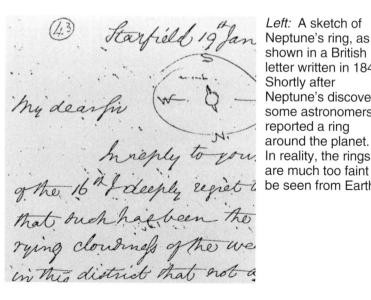

Left: A sketch of Neptune's ring, as shown in a British letter written in 1847. Shortly after Neptune's discovery, some astronomers reported a ring around the planet. In reality, the rings are much too faint to be seen from Earth.

Of rings we sing!

There are four giant planets in the Solar System, and each of them has rings. The rings of Jupiter, Uranus, and Neptune are all thin, faint, and made up of dark particles — pieces of rock and ice — that cannot be seen clearly from Earth. Space probes proved these rings exist. Saturn has many broad rings made of bright particles, and these rings can be seen from Earth through binoculars or a small telescope. The mystery is not why planets have rings, but why Saturn alone has such magnificent rings.

The clumps in Neptune's rings are seen in this *Voyager 2* picture.

Violent Winds

On Earth, winds are powered by the Sun's heat. Since Neptune is farther from the Sun than Jupiter, it receives less heat than Jupiter — only 3 percent as much. For this reason, astronomers expected Neptune's atmosphere to be much quieter than Jupiter's, which has powerful winds. *Voyager 2* found, however, that the winds of Neptune are surprisingly violent. They move at speeds as high as 1,200 miles (2,000 km) per hour — the highest speeds in the Solar System. Scientists are not sure why Neptune has such strong winds. Perhaps heat from inside the planet helps power them. Jupiter produces more heat than Neptune, though, so why doesn't it have stronger winds?

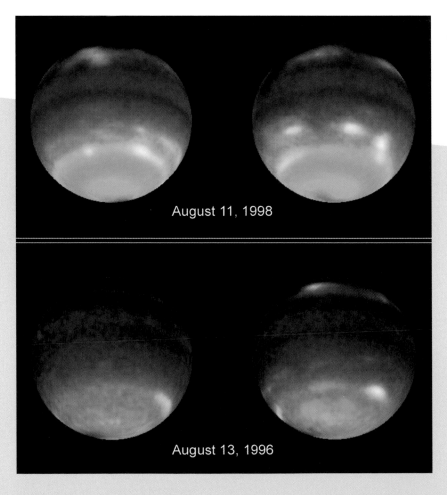

August 11, 1998

August 13, 1996

Left: Using telescopic observations from both the Hubble Space Telescope and NASA's Infrared Telescope Facility in Hawaii, scientists have captured these images of Neptune's surface.

In this drawing, Neptune's atmosphere distorts and multiplies the image of the setting Sun.

Neptune — one far-out planet!

Neptune takes almost 165 years to orbit the Sun, so it has not yet completed a single orbit since its discovery in 1846. It will not come back to the place where it was first seen until 2011. Pluto, which takes about 250 years to orbit the Sun, is usually the farthest known planet. During a 20-year period in Pluto's orbit, however, it is a bit closer than Neptune to the Sun. This happened most recently between 1979 and 1999. During those years, Neptune was the farthest planet from the Sun.

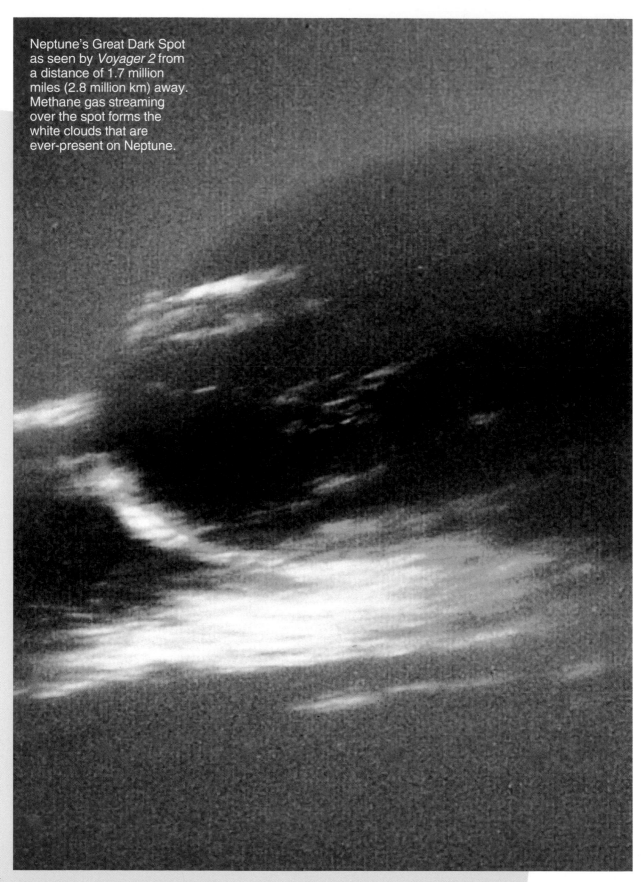

Neptune's Great Dark Spot as seen by *Voyager 2* from a distance of 1.7 million miles (2.8 million km) away. Methane gas streaming over the spot forms the white clouds that are ever-present on Neptune.

Neptune's Great Surprise

Voyager 2 showed that Neptune is full of surprises. Perhaps *Voyager*'s most astonishing discovery was that Neptune had something in its atmosphere that was like the Great Red Spot on Jupiter.

Like Jupiter's red spot, Neptune's dark spot seemed to be a gigantic storm pattern. It had the same shape as Jupiter's spot. Neptune's spot was deep blue in color, however, with a slight reddish tint. Although its width was as big as Earth's diameter, the Great Dark Spot was smaller than Jupiter's spot. If Neptune were scaled up to be the same size as Jupiter, however, the spots would be the same size, too.

Mysteriously, when the Hubble Space Telescope observed Neptune a few years after *Voyager*, the planet's Great Dark Spot had disappeared. Scientists do not know why Neptune's big spot vanished.

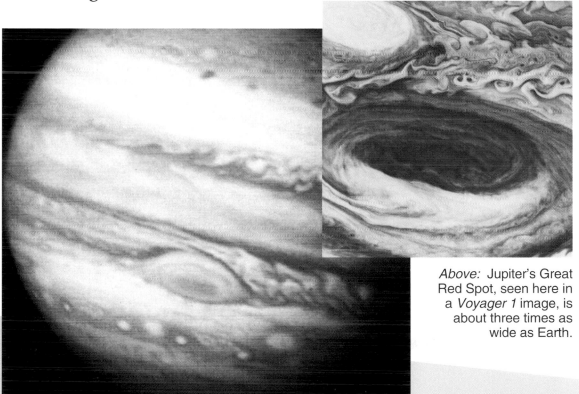

Above: Jupiter's Great Red Spot, seen here in a *Voyager 1* image, is about three times as wide as Earth.

Above: Jupiter's Great Red Spot is clearly visible in the planet's Southern Hemisphere. Neptune's dark spot was strikingly similar to it.

17

Planetary Magnetism

Jupiter has a magnetic field that is much stronger than Earth's. Saturn and Uranus have magnetic fields, and *Voyager 2* detected a magnetic field around Neptune, as well. In order to have a magnetic field, a gaseous giant planet must have a liquid region somewhere in its interior that conducts electricity. On the whole, Neptune seems like the other giant planets. It is made up mostly of gaseous substances that get hot and dense in the interior. It may have a small rocky core surrounded by a liquid layer. Some scientists think the source of Neptune's magnetic field may be closer to its surface than to its core.

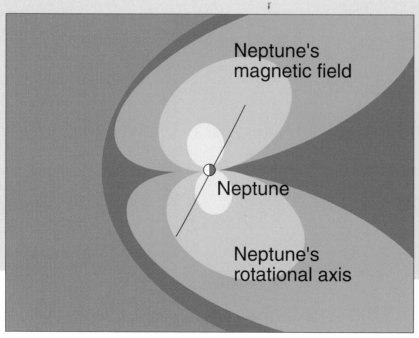

Neptune's magnetic field

Neptune

Neptune's rotational axis

Left: Voyager scientists were surprised to learn how far the axis of Neptune's magnetic field tilts away from the axis of the planet's rotation. The magnetic field also seems to be centered on a spot some distance from Neptune's center. *Voyager 2* showed that Neptune's magnetic field is similar to that of Uranus – and very different from Earth's.

The case of the tipped magnetic fields

According to scientists, a celestial body's magnetic field ought to line up with the body's axis of rotation. For some reason, Earth's magnetic field tips a little bit toward its axis. Uranus's magnetic field tips way over. Uranus's axis is turned so the planet seems to be rolling on its side. This might be why its magnetic field is so tilted. Neptune's axis is much more upright, and yet its magnetic field is greatly tipped, too. Why? Scientists are not sure.

Scientists think Neptune may have a rocky core surrounded by a liquid layer and, higher up, a gaseous "envelope." Its atmosphere consists of hydrogen, helium, and smaller amounts of other gases, such as methane, which is believed to be largely responsible for the planet's blue color. The enlarged section shows cloud layers in the upper part of Neptune's stormy atmosphere.

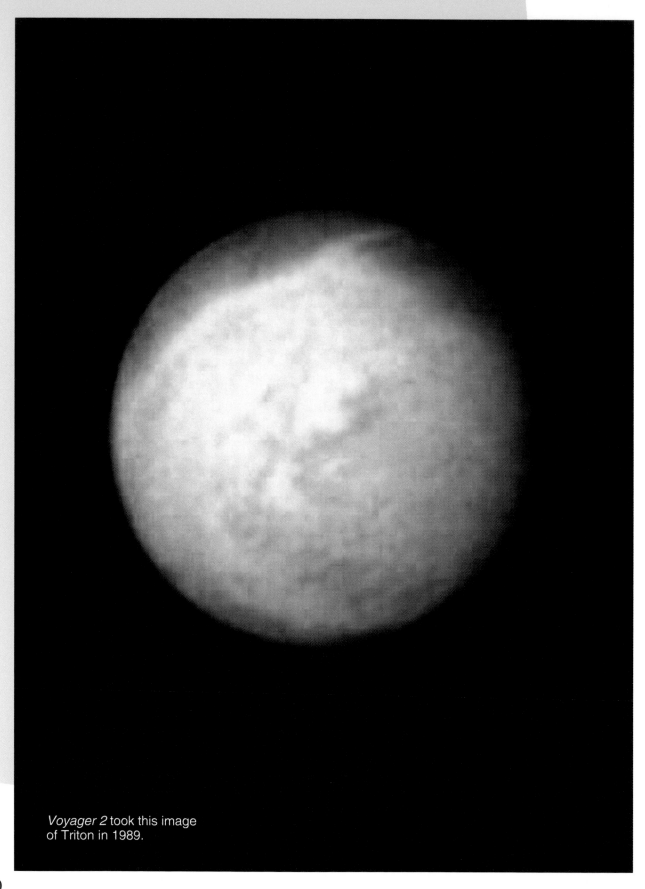

Voyager 2 took this image
of Triton in 1989.

Triton — Neptune's Largest Moon

Voyager 2 passed near Triton, Neptune's largest satellite. Triton's diameter is about 1,680 miles (2,700 km). That is about 3/4 as wide as Earth's Moon, which is about 2,160 miles (3,475 km) across.

Some scientists expected Triton to be similar to Saturn's large satellite, Titan. Titan is large enough to hold a hazy atmosphere that hides its surface. Triton, however, has only a very thin atmosphere, composed mainly of nitrogen, and its surface is clearly visible.

Left: The surface of Titan, Saturn's largest moon, hides beneath a hazy atmosphere of nitrogen and other gases, such as methane.

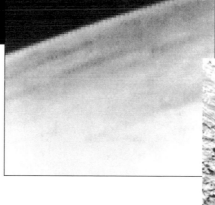

Left: Triton's thin atmosphere suspends icy particles that form a thin haze around the moon.

Right: Circular depressions on Triton may be caused by the melting and collapsing of the moon's icy surface.

Wrong-way Triton — a captured asteroid?

Most moons move around their planet in the same direction as the planet turns on its axis. Six of the Solar System's seven largest moons, including Earth's Moon, move in the normal direction, west to east. The exception is Triton. Neptune rotates west to east as Earth does, but Triton moves around Neptune east to west. Could Triton be an asteroid or comet that was captured by Neptune's gravity? Scientists do not know for sure.

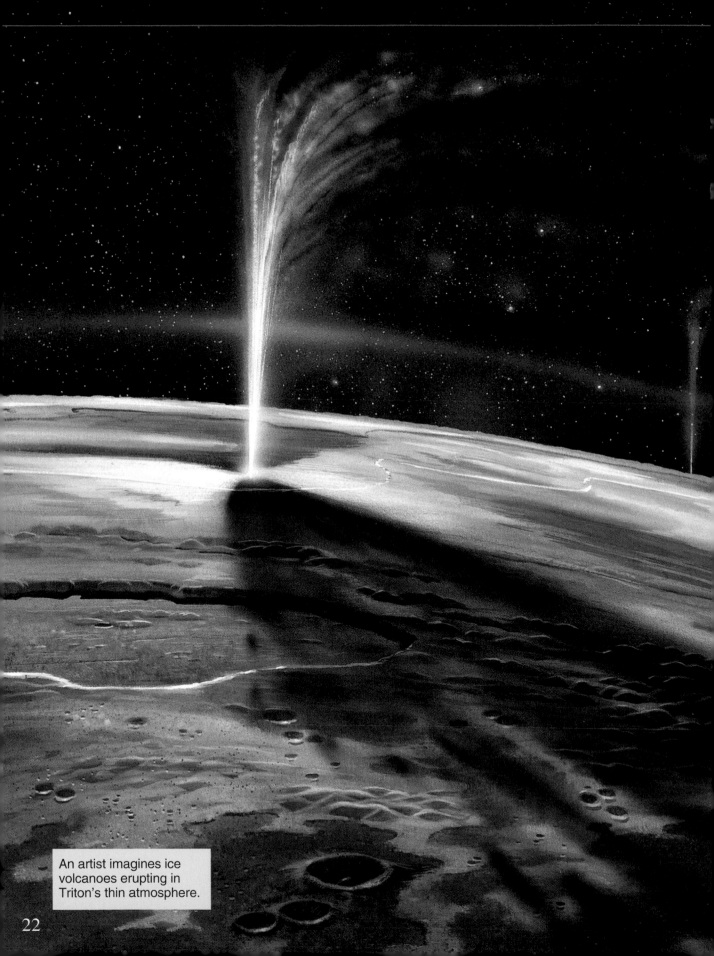

An artist imagines ice
volcanoes erupting in
Triton's thin atmosphere.

22

Triton's Ice Volcanoes

Triton's surface is an icy landscape of frozen nitrogen. This frozen surface reflects sunlight well, so Triton is much brighter than the other moons of Neptune. Triton is the coldest Solar System body yet observed, with temperatures as low as -390° Fahrenheit (-235° Centigrade). Triton's south polar ice cap looks pink. Scientists think some of the color may come from methane ice.

Nitrogen ice may allow the feeble sunlight to reach deep layers of Triton's crust. Once warmed by sunlight, these deep layers cannot quickly cool because the nitrogen ice above will not let infrared radiation escape as easily as it lets light in. Scientists think this may be the source of energy for Triton's biggest surprise — ice volcanoes that throw a mixture of nitrogen, methane, and other substances high above the frigid surface.

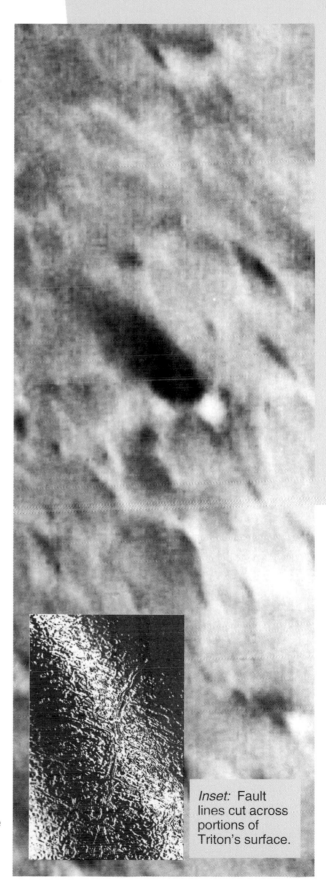

Right: Dark streaks pepper the surface of Triton's south polar cap. They may be the result of material being shot into the atmosphere by ice volcanoes. *Voyager 2* observed such eruptions in progress – the plumes of the geysers reached a height of perhaps 5 miles (8 km). The sources of a couple of eruptions are seen as circular white spots in this photo.

Inset: Fault lines cut across portions of Triton's surface.

Captured Comets

Triton's odd orbit leads some scientists to think that it formed elsewhere and was later captured by Neptune.

Indeed, astronomers have discovered dozens of large comet- and asteroid-like bodies lying beyond Neptune.

Some scientists call them "plutinos" because they may be the kinds of objects from which Pluto was formed.

Pluto's own moon, Charon, more closely resembles the moons of Saturn than it does Pluto, however.

Above: Johann Gottfried Galle shared in Neptune's discovery.

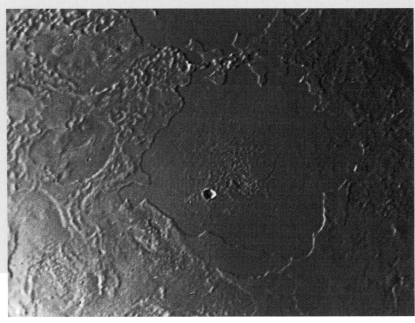

Above: Voyager 2 provided the best glimpse of Triton, so far. A single crater about 8 miles (13 km) wide can be seen near the center of this view. The large flat depression around it may be the remains of an older larger crater filled in by the thick ice lavas that have reshaped Triton's surface. The rough area in the center of the depression may mark a recent eruption.

Sometimes two wrongs do make a right!

When Adams and Leverrier calculated Neptune's position, they did not know how far beyond Uranus it might be. Each incorrectly guessed that Neptune was much farther away and much larger than it really is. These two mistakes canceled each other, and each man ended up predicting that Neptune would be where it actually is.

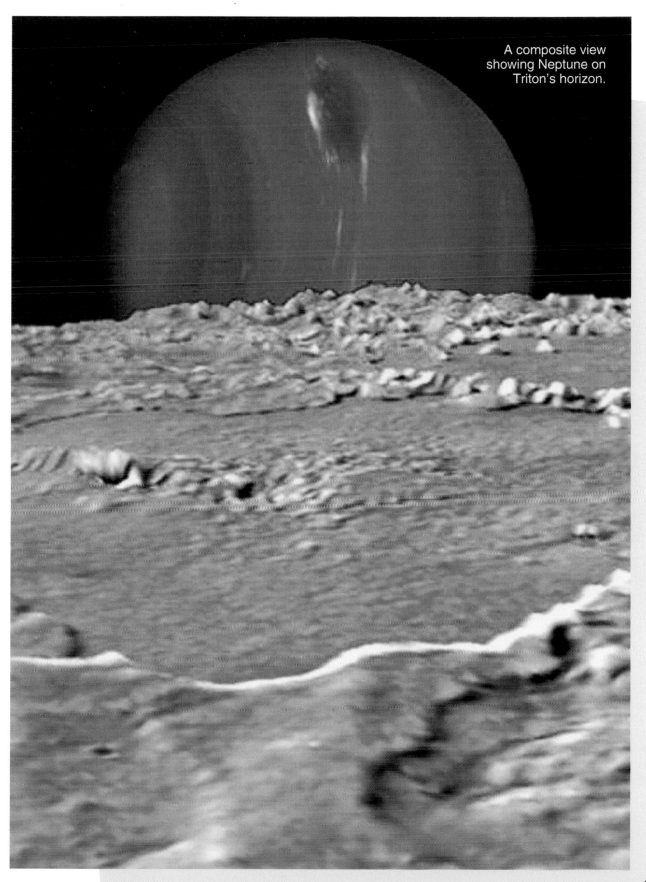

A composite view showing Neptune on Triton's horizon.

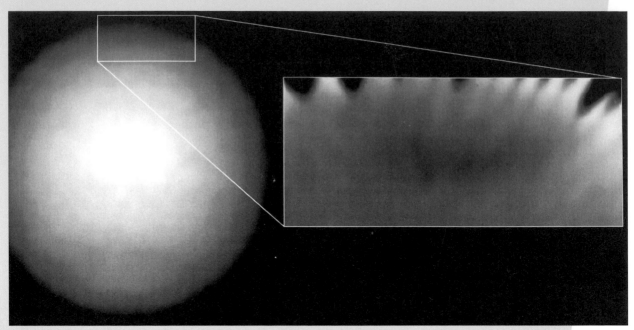

Above: Scientists studying Neptune with the Hubble Space Telescope in 1994 were surprised to find not only that the Great Dark Spot seen by *Voyager 2* had disappeared, but also that a similar spot had formed in the opposite hemisphere.

Voyager 2's farewell photograph of Neptune and Triton, both slender crescents from the spacecraft's viewpoint.

A Journey of Discovery — *Voyager 2*

Scientists have traced the path *Voyager 2* will follow for the next million years. By then, it will be 50 light-years away, about twelve times farther away than the nearest star other than our Sun. In all the time it takes to travel that far, *Voyager* will never meet up with another star. Its closest approach to any star other than our Sun will be no closer than 1.65 light-years, almost 10 trillion miles (16 trillion km).

Scientists do not know what surprises await *Voyager* as it sails through the cosmos. For now, Neptune holds the prize for the most news beamed back home by *Voyager*.

Until we can send a spacecraft to Neptune again, the Hubble Space Telescope and other instruments will supply scientists with additional data. Hubble can see features in Neptune's cloud tops that are 620 miles (1,000 km) across. The Hubble has already served up a puzzle for planetary scientists.

When *Voyager 2* passed Neptune in 1989, its cameras revealed the Great Dark Spot in the planet's Southern Hemisphere. Yet Hubble images taken in late 1994 indicated that the Great Dark Spot had vanished and that a new dark spot had appeared in Neptune's Northern Hemisphere. Scientists do not quite understand what is going on in Neptune's atmosphere.

Fact File: A Distant Giant

Neptune is our Solar System's fourth-largest known planet. It is the eighth-farthest planet from the Sun. Only tiny Pluto has an orbit that stretches farther from the Sun. In fact, Neptune is so far from the Sun that its year equals nearly 165 Earth years. For about twenty of those years, Pluto's unusual orbit comes within Neptune's orbit. This means that Neptune is then farther from the Sun than Pluto.

With the journey of *Voyager 2* past Neptune in 1989, and with later observations made by the Hubble Space Telescope, many mysteries about this cold and beautiful planet were solved, and many previously unknown secrets were revealed.

Stay tuned for more as scientists continue their studies of this magnificent distant giant called Neptune.

Left: Neptune and its moons.

The Moons of Neptune

Name	Triton	Nereid	Proteus	Larissa
Diameter	1,680 miles (2,700 km)	210 miles (340 km)	260 miles (420 km)	120 miles (190 km)
Distance from Neptune	220,300 miles (354,800 km)	3,424,000 miles (5,513,000 km)	73,000 miles (117,600 km)	457,000 miles (73,600 km)

Name	Despina	Galatea	Thalassa	Naiad
Diameter	90 miles (145 km)	100 miles (160 km)	50 miles (80 km)	35 miles (60 km)
Distance from Neptune	32,600 miles (52,500 km)	38,500 miles (62,000 km)	31,000 miles (50,000 km)	30,000 miles (48,200 km)

Neptune: How It Measures Up to Earth

Planet	Diameter	Rotation Period (length of day)	Period of Orbit around Sun (length of year)	Known Moons	Surface Gravity
Neptune	30,760 miles (49,500 km)	16 hours, 7 minutes	164 years 288 days	8	1.12*
Earth	7,927 miles (12,756 km)	23 hours, 56 minutes	365.25 days (1 year)	1	1.00*

* Multiply your weight by this number to find out how much you would weigh on this planet. In the case of Neptune, which lacks a surface, the number is for cloud-top level.

Planet	Distance from Sun (nearest–farthest)	Least Time It Takes for Light to Travel to Earth
Neptune	2.76–2.83 billion miles (4.44–4.55 billion km)	3 hours, 59 minutes —
Earth	91.3–94.4 million miles (147–152 million km)	— —

Neptune

The Sun and its Solar System family (*left to right):* Mercury, Venus, Earth, Mars, Jupiter, Saturn, Uranus, Neptune, and Pluto.

More Books about Neptune

DK Space Encyclopedia. Nigel Henbest and Heather Couper (DK Publishing)

Jupiter, Saturn, Uranus, and Neptune. Gregory Vogt (Raintree Steck-Vaughn)

Neptune. Larry Dane Brimner (Children's Press)

Neptune. Seymour Simon (Mulberry Books)

CD-ROMs and DVDs

CD-ROM: *Exploring the Planets.* (Cinegram)

DVD: *The Voyager Odyssey: An Interplanetary Music Video Experience.* (Image Entertainment)

Web Sites

The Internet is a good place to get more information about Neptune. The web sites listed here can help you learn about the most recent discoveries, as well as those made in the past.

Nine Planets. www.nineplanets.org/neptune.html

StarDate Online. stardate.org/resources/ssguide/neptune.html

Views of the Solar System. www.solarviews.com/eng/neptune.htm

Voyager Project Home Page. voyager.jpl.nasa.gov/

Windows to the Universe. www.windows.ucar.edu/tour/link=/neptune/neptune.html

Places to Visit

Here are some museums and centers where you can find a variety of space exhibits.

American Museum of Natural History
Central Park West at 79th Street
New York, NY 10024

Canada Science and Technology Museum
1867 St. Laurent Boulevard
Science Park
100 Queen's Park
Ottawa, Ontario K1G 5A3
Canada

National Air and Space Museum
Smithsonian Institution
7th and Independence Avenue SW
Washington, DC 20560

Odyssium
11211 142nd Street
Edmonton, Alberta T5M 4A1
Canada

Scienceworks Museum
2 Booker Street
Spotswood
Melbourne, Victoria 3015
Australia

U.S. Space and Rocket Center
1 Tranquility Base
Huntsville, AL 35807

Glossary

asteroids: very small "planets." There are hundreds of thousands of them in our Solar System. Most of them orbit the Sun between Mars and Jupiter, but many occur elsewhere. Some asteroids come close to Earth. Some moons of Neptune and other planets may be "captured" asteroids.

atmosphere: the gases surrounding a planet, star, or moon. Neptune's atmosphere contains hydrogen, helium, and other gases.

axis: the imaginary straight line around which a planet, star, or moon turns or rotates.

comet: a small object in space made of ice, rock, and gas. It has a vapor tail that can be seen from Earth when the comet's orbit brings it close to the Sun.

gravity: the force that causes objects like Earth and the Moon to be drawn toward one another.

Great Dark Spot: a big dark storm pattern shaped like an oval that was observed by the *Voyager 2* probe in Neptune's Southern Hemisphere in 1989.

Great Red Spot: a huge reddish-colored oval storm pattern in Jupiter's Southern Hemisphere that has lasted for centuries.

Hubble Space Telescope: an artificial satellite containing a telescope and related instruments that was placed in orbit around Earth in 1990.

light-year: the distance that light travels in one year – nearly six trillion miles (9.6 trillion km).

methane: a colorless, odorless, flammable gas.

moon: a small body in space that moves in an orbit around a larger body. A moon is said to be a satellite of the larger body. Neptune has eight known moons, the largest of which is called Triton.

NASA: the government space agency in the United States. Its full name is the National Aeronautics and Space Administration.

nitrogen: a chemical element that at sufficiently warm temperatures occurs as a colorless, odorless gas. It is found in the atmospheres of Earth and Neptune's moon, Triton.

orbit: the path that one celestial object follows as it circles, or revolves, around another.

probe: a craft that travels in space, photographing and studying celestial bodies and in some cases even landing on them.

Solar System: the Sun with the planets and all the other bodies, such as the asteroids, that orbit the Sun.

Sun: our star and the provider of the energy that makes life possible on Earth.

Triton: Neptune's largest moon. It has its own atmosphere and is bigger than the planet Pluto.

Voyager: the name of two U.S. space probes that were launched in 1977. Both *Voyager 1* and *Voyager 2* later flew by Jupiter and Saturn. *Voyager 2* also flew by Uranus (in 1986) and Neptune (in 1989).

Index

Born in 1920, Isaac Asimov came to the United States as a young boy from his native Russia. As a young man, he was a student of biochemistry. In time, he became one of the most productive writers the world has ever known. His books cover a spectrum of topics, including science, history, language theory, fantasy, and science fiction. His brilliant imagination gained him the respect and admiration of adults and children alike. Sadly, Isaac Asimov died shortly after the publication of the first edition of *Isaac Asimov's Library of the Universe.*

The publishers wish to thank the following for permission to reproduce copyright material: front cover, 3, 20, 25, 27, National Space Science Data Center and the Team Leader, Dr. Bradford A. Smith; 4, National Space Science Data Center; 5 (both), Yerkes Observatory; 6, Sharon Burris/© Gareth Stevens, Inc.; 7 (large), Jet Propulsion Laboratory; 7 (inset), NASA; 8, Sharon Burris/© Gareth Stevens, Inc.; 9 (large), Yerkes Observatory; 9 (inset), Jet Propulsion Laboratory; 10 (upper, lower), Jet Propulsion Laboratory; 10 (inset), Courtesy P. J. Stooke, University of Western Ontario; 11, Jet Propulsion Laboratory; 12, Collection of Richard Baum; 13, Jet Propulsion Laboratory; 14, Lawrence A. Sromovsky (University of Wisconsin-Madison) and NASA; 15, © Sally Bensusen 1989; 16, Jet Propulsion Laboratory; 17 (both), NASA; 18, Sharon Burris/© Gareth Stevens, Inc.; 19, © Paul Dimare 1989; 21 (all), Jet Propulsion Laboratory; 22, © Paul Dimare 1989; 23 (both), Jet Propulsion Laboratory; 24 (left), Yerkes Observatory; 24 (right), Jet Propulsion Laboratory; 26 (upper), H. Hammel (Massachusetts Institute of Technology) and NASA; 26 (lower), Jet Propulsion Laboratory; 28, © Thomas O. Miller/Studio "X," 1990; 28-29, © Sally Bensusen.